I TOO HAD A STORY

Sheetal Agrawal

BookLeaf Publishing

India | USA | UK

Presentation by *BookLeaf Publishing*

Web: www.bookleafpub.com

E-mail: info@bookleafpub.com

ISBN: 9789363312173

First edition 2024

To the resilient souls who have shared their stories with me, and to those who navigate their own journeys with courage and grace.

To my family, whose love and support have been my foundation.

To my friends, whose companionship has brightened my path.

To my brother Rahul Agrawal and my bhabhi Bhini Agrawal, whose unwavering belief in me has been my guiding star.

To my sister-in-law Shewta Agarwal and her family, for your warmth and kindness.

And to the special angel whose unseen guidance has been a constant source of strength.

*This book is dedicated to all of you, with
immense gratitude and love. Thank you for
being a part of my story.*

ACKNOWLEDGEMENT

As I reflect on the journey of creating *I Too Had a Story*, I am filled with gratitude for the many people who have been a part of this process. While the path has not always been easy, I have learned valuable lessons along the way.

To my husband, your presence in my life has been a complex and multifaceted journey. Through our shared experiences, both positive and challenging, I have learned lessons that have shaped me as a person and as a writer. Your influence, while not without its struggles, has pushed me to grow and find my voice.

To my family members, your encouragement and love have been my greatest source of strength. You have shaped who I am today, and I am forever grateful for your presence in my life.

To all the individuals who have been a part of these stories, your trust in sharing your experiences with me has allowed these narratives to come alive on the page. Thank you for opening your hearts and minds, and for allowing me to bring your stories to light.

To my friends, your companionship and support have meant the world to me. You have been there through every high and low, and I am thankful for your enduring friendship.

Special thanks to my brother Rahul Agrawal and my bhabhi Bhini Agrawal. Your love and guidance have been a guiding light on this journey. Your belief in me has been instrumental in bringing this book to life.

To my sister-in-law, Shewta Agarwal and her family, thank you for your warmth and kindness. Your support has been invaluable in this endeavor.

I also want to express my deepest gratitude to a special angel, whose quiet support and unseen guidance have been my saving grace. Though your identity may remain a mystery, your presence has touched my life in profound ways. Thank you for your steadfast belief in my journey.

With heartfelt thanks,

Sheetal Agrawal

PREFACE

In writing *I Too Had a Story*, I set out on a journey to capture the mosaic of human experiences that shape our lives. This collection of narratives is a tribute to the resilience and complexity of the human spirit, as seen through the lens of ordinary people facing extraordinary circumstances. Each story is a snapshot of a life lived, with its own unique challenges, dreams, and moments of grace.

The characters within these pages represent a diverse array of voices and backgrounds, yet they all share one common thread: their stories resonate with the universal themes of love, loss, hope, and perseverance. Through their journeys, we come to understand that our struggles and joys, though deeply personal, are also part of a shared human experience.

As you read these stories, I invite you to reflect on your own journey and the stories you carry within. May these narratives inspire you to embrace your own path with courage and compassion, and to recognize the beauty and strength that resides in each of us.

I am deeply grateful to have had the opportunity to bring these stories to life, and I hope they touch your heart as much as they have touched mine. Thank you for joining me on this literary journey.

With gratitude,

Sheetal Agrawal

A Daughter's Arrival

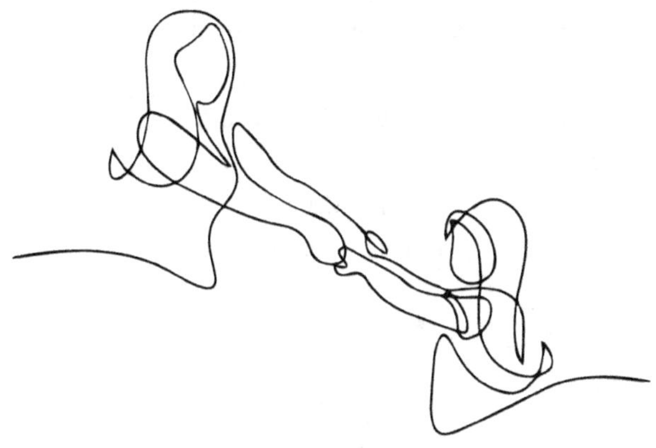

After years of waiting, a miracle unfolds,
A tiny heartbeat, a new story told.
Joy fills the air, as dawn starts anew,
A daughter has come, life's dreams to pursue.

The years of longing now find their rest,
As she enters the world, the family's blessed.
Faces light up, like the morning sun,
Her first cry heard, the journey begun.

A mother's tears, a father's pride,
Their hearts entwined with joy inside.
The home now dances with laughter and cheer,
A daughter's presence, precious and dear.

Petals of hope blossom in her wake,
A new chapter written, the past she breaks.
Struggles forgotten, in her gentle glow,
She brings a warmth only parents know.

A promise of love, a gift from above,
The family's world wrapped in a glove.
A daughter's arrival, a dream come true,
A whisper of light in skies once blue.

Days of Wonder

In the halls of youth, where dreams take flight,
She walks with a spirit, shining so bright.
Curiosity sparkles in her wide-eyed gaze,
Her school days, a journey through life's gentle
maze.

In the classroom, she sits with an open mind,
Learning and questioning, answers to find.
Her voice, a song, sharing thoughts aloud,
In a sea of children, she stands so proud.

Recess brings laughter, games in the sun,
With friends she's made, her heart has won.
Adventures unfold on the playground's stage,
In her world of wonder, she's center stage.

Books are her companions, whispering tales,
Of faraway lands and ships with sails.
She loses herself in each story's embrace,
As imagination takes her to a magical place.

Challenges arise, yet she faces them strong,
With courage and heart, she finds where she
belongs.
Teachers inspire her, guiding her way,

To dream of tomorrow and seize today.

The years pass by, her spirit grows,
Her path is clear, as she faces new woes.
In her school days, she finds her stride,
A journey of learning with hope as her guide.

As she steps into the world beyond,
Her school days remain a cherished bond.
With memories bright, and heart aglow,
She carries the lessons that helped her grow.

A Dreamer's Journey

On the train, the world rushes past,
Dreams of white coats and futures vast.
In her heart, a steady beat,
A doctor's path, so bittersweet.

Her first proposal, a whisper soft,
Yet her focus held, her dreams aloft.
A gentle touch, yet she stood her ground,
Her goals in sight, her heart unbound.

In lecture halls, she took her place,
While friends would wander, leave no trace.
Her notes were meticulous, her mind alive,
In the world of medicine, she would thrive.

The lure of freedom called her name,
But she stayed true, her course the same.
No chance to chill with friends she knew,
Her dedication held, her dreams in view.

Economic trials tested her soul,
Yet she pressed on, her eye on the goal.
She learned to bend, but not to break,
Her journey one she would never forsake.

Through challenges faced, her spirit grew,
A steadfast strength, a heart so true.
Her college days, a path of light,
Guiding her through the darkest night.

A dreamer's journey, full of grace,
She walks her path with measured pace.
A doctor's heart, her vision clear,
Her future bright, her soul sincere.

A Dream Set Aside

The day she received the news so sweet,
A dream she'd chased, now at her feet.
Admission to medicine, her heart took flight,
A future of healing, within her sight.

But shadows loomed from within her home,
A world of pressure, where dreams couldn't
roam.
Family's wishes, traditions tight,
Orthodox views dimmed her light.

The call to heal, a path so pure,
Yet she faced a struggle she had to endure.
A choice not her own, but one she must face,
Her dreams set aside, with grace and pace.

Microbiology became her next quest,
A new path chosen, she gave her best.
In the world of microbes, she sought to excel,
Yet a piece of her dream within her fell.

Resilience grew in her quiet soul,
As she adjusted to the unexpected toll.
Her passion for learning did not wane,
Despite the heartache, she bore the pain.

With each step taken, she found her way,
Though her first dream had gone astray.
A strength within, she carried on,
Her spirit resilient, her will not gone.

Though medicine's path she could not embrace,
She held her head high with dignity and grace.
Her journey continued, a different view,
A story of courage, her heart stayed true.

A Triumph Unseen

In her final year, she shone so bright,
Her passion and knowledge guiding her right.
In microbiology, she reached the peak,
Topping her class, her future unique.

Her achievements celebrated far and wide,
A scholar of grace, with talent and pride.
Her heart soared high, her dreams took flight,
A path to success, within her sight.

Yet whispers of tradition filled her home,
A choice awaited, she couldn't roam.
Post-graduation, a door now closed,
As marriage became the path she chose.

Her dreams of further study set aside,
For a life with a husband by her side.
She faced the world with a quiet strength,
Her spirit steady, going to any length.

The world around her could not see,
The fire within her, her silent plea.
For a dream put on hold, a chance denied,
Her journey altered, yet not her pride.

Despite the hurdles she did endure,
Her resilience and grace remained pure.
Though her path was not as she once planned,
She faced the future, steady and grand.

A triumph unseen by many's gaze,
Yet her heart remained, in its own ways.
For she knew her worth, her spirit strong,
Her journey continuing, where she belongs.

A Love That Blooms

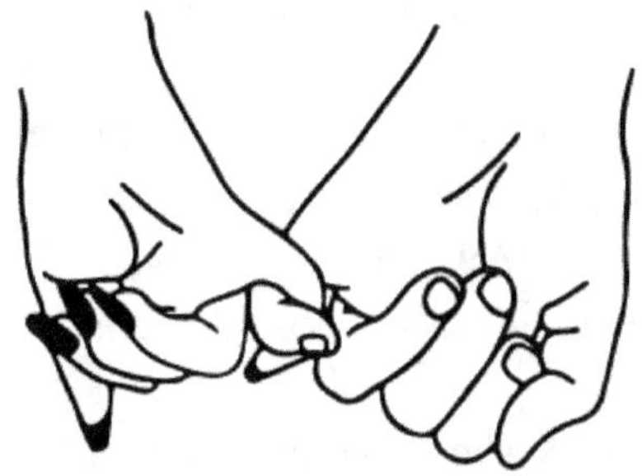

In the quiet courtship, her heart took flight,
A journey of dreams in the soft moonlight.
With gentle words and promises sweet,
Two souls entwined, their hearts to meet.

His support a beacon, lighting her way,
In her dreams of studies, he stood to say:
"Chase your passions, follow your quest,
Together we'll face every test."

Her dreams of healing, once set aside,
Now found new hope with him by her side.
The future she longed for, clear as day,
With him beside her, she found her way.

In his embrace, her doubts would fade,
His love a shelter, a quiet glade.
For the first time, her heart felt whole,
As love began to nourish her soul.

Her dreams took root, a garden of grace,
With him, she found her special place.
Their laughter echoed in the night,
Their shared hopes shining so bright.

In her studies, she found new delight,
With his faith in her, she soared to new heights.
Together they'd build a life so true,
With love as the foundation, in all they do.

For the first time, she loved someone deep,
A love that promised, a love to keep.
Her journey now filled with warmth and light,
With him by her side, her future felt right.

Once a month, their worlds align,
A day of joy, where hearts entwine.
In shared moments, laughter's song,
A bond unbreakable, together strong.

A love that blooms, a dream come true,
Her heart now full, her skies all blue.
Together they walk, hand in hand,
A journey of love, a dreamer and her man.

Silent Struggles: Early Days of Marriage

In the early days of marriage, her world grew small,
Confined within the four walls, answering each call.
She tended to chores, from dawn till dusk,
Her dreams set aside, her heart a quiet husk.

Each day demanded much, expectations high,
Her spirit tested under the watchful eye.
The weight of traditions pressed on her soul,
The pressure of motherhood taking its toll.

She bore the weight of unspoken demand,
The hope of a child, as families planned.
Her own desires buried deep within,
Her journey now shaped by others' whims.

The once-bright dreams now dimmed and
veiled,
In the world of her home, her ambitions
curtailed.
She moved with grace through each demanding
task,
Hiding her wishes behind a poised mask.
Though her heart longed for more than this,
She held on tightly to dreams she couldn't
dismiss.
Her early days of marriage, a silent fight,
As she navigated her world, her own dreams in
sight.

In the new house, she walked with care,
Learning the ways, the customs there.
A culture different, traditions unknown,
In a world that was not quite her own.

Calls to her family, a rare delight,
Limited by expectations, kept out of sight.
Visits to home were precious and few,
A bittersweet joy in moments she knew.

She treaded softly, her heart kept still,
Adjusting her life to fit their will.
New norms to follow, old ways to bend,
A journey of blending, where change had no
end.

The new traditions she learned to embrace,
Though her heart longed for her family's grace.
She carried the weight of her new life's
demands,
Navigating the changes with careful hands.

Amidst the unfamiliar, she found her way,
Striving to honor each role she must play.
Though her own roots felt distant and far,
She held her strength, her guiding star.

The Silent Descent

Each month she faced the unknown,
Painful procedures, her heart alone.
The hope she carried, a heavy weight,
As she endured the trials of fate.

Needles and tests, her body weary,
Yet she pressed on, her vision teary.
The sadness that followed each failed result,
A deep ache within, no words could halt.

The whispers of tradition filled the air,
With superstitions she must bear.
A childless home, a curse they said,
Her spirit bowed under the dread.

The cost of treatment weighed on her soul,
Monetary burdens taking their toll.
Yet she fought on, her dreams unshaken,
Her desire to be a mother never forsaken.

In temples, mosques, and churches she prayed,
A quest for solace, her faith displayed.
In every shrine, a wish she whispered,
For the child she yearned for, her heart so
blistered.

In shadows she hides the pain within,
Forced to endure, a heavy sin.
Medications change her, her body's plight,
Weight she carries, mood swings at night.

Through whispers of duty, she silences her
voice,
Each encounter a loss of her own choice.
The burden of expectations, a heavy load,
She bears the strain on her lonely road.

Medications seep, altering her form,
A body once vibrant, now weathering the storm.
Her emotions a tempest, mood swings untamed,
She navigates this path, her spirit unclaimed.

The mirror reflects a stranger's face,
A body transformed, a loss of grace.

Yet she carries on, through nights so bleak,
Longing for dreams she dares not speak.

The weight of the journey leaves scars deep,
Her heart heavy with secrets she keeps.
Though pain and sadness haunt her sleep,
She moves forward, through shadows so steep.
The journey was long, the path unsure,
Her hope a flame, fragile and pure.
Through it all, she held on tight,
A mother's dream in the darkest night.

Though her struggles were often unseen,
Her heart remained a place serene.
A silent descent through trials so rough,
A mother's journey, her dream enough.

A Miracle Unveiled

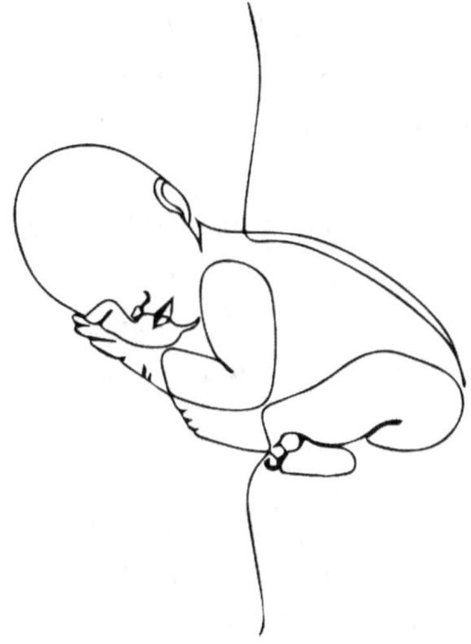

The day dawned bright with hope anew,
A whisper of change, a dream come true.
In her heart, a fluttering beat,
As the news she longed for felt so sweet.

The test in her hands, her breath held tight,
A moment of prayer, her soul alight.
As she saw the signs, her eyes filled with tears,
The answer she sought for so many years.

A rush of joy, a wave of relief,
A miracle blooming, dissolving her grief.
The journey ahead, a path uncharted,
But in this moment, her dream had started.

Her heart now danced with a rhythm pure,
A life within, her hope's allure.
The burden of waiting, now set aside,
She embraced the news with swelling pride.

A smile spread wide, a light in her eyes,
Her heart soared high, touching the skies.
The news of her child, a precious delight,
Filled her with joy, a newfound might.

The weight of the past, lifted away,
Replaced by dreams of a brighter day.
She could see the future, a family complete,
A life she'd imagined, now at her feet.

Whispers of hope danced on the breeze,
A mother's love starting to seize.
The warmth of new beginnings embraced her,
A glow of life within, her heart's stir.

Tears of joy streamed down her face,
A victory over pain, a sacred grace.
She held the news close, a treasure to keep,
A moment of triumph, her soul to leap.

Her journey now found its golden reward,
The news of a child, her heart's accord.
A story of dreams, a chapter so bright,

The day she knew everything was right.

The world around her seemed to glow,
A future of promise, a love to grow.
In this moment, her world was complete,
The day she first heard her child's heartbeat.

Endurance and Love: A Mother's Journey

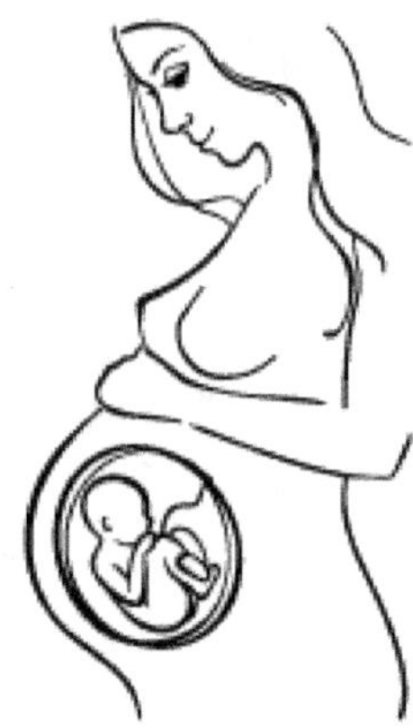

After the first three months, her world grew still,
A time of challenge, a test of her will.
Bed rest commanded, her body to mend,
Her daily routines came to an abrupt end.

Work put aside, her dreams on hold,
Family's response, not as she was told.
Their lack of support weighed on her heart,
In her silent struggle, she stood apart.

Proper food, a scarcity faced,
Her nourishment lost, her strength misplaced.
Yet each month her mother came near,
Bringing the food she held so dear.

A taste of comfort, a mother's care,
In her small sanctuary, love filled the air.
Though life's hardships burdened her soul,
She held on tight to her ultimate goal.

For the child within, she bore the pain,
Her sacrifices never made in vain.
A mother's resolve, a heart full of grace,
To protect her child, she faced the chase.
Through nights of longing and days of strain,
She whispered to the life within her domain.
Though the road was rough, she never lost sight,
For the love of her child, she'd endure any
plight.

Each month brought a new, daunting fight,
Hospital rooms, a familiar sight.
Complications plagued her fragile frame,
Her journey fraught with trials untamed.

Her weight climbed high, a heavy load,
Ninety-eight kilograms, her body showed.
Swelling took hold, her hands and feet,
A constant reminder of battles to meet.

Through hospital doors, she entered in fear,
Yet her love for her child held her near.
Each stay a challenge, her strength put to test,

Yet she fought on, for she knew best.

Her swollen limbs, a burden she bore,
Yet in her heart, she longed for more.
A hope for the day she would finally see,
The child she cherished, her destiny.

The path was rough, her spirit weary,
Yet she pressed on, her vision clear.
In the face of hardship, she would not bend,
Her love for her child, her guiding friend.

Though her body ached and her heart was sore,
Her will unwavering, she would endure.
For her child within, she stood her ground,
A mother's love, the truest sound.

A Mother's Unyielding Resolve

For ten long hours, she battled the pain,
Labour's relentless, harsh, unchained.
Then the doctors spoke of a critical turn,
A C-section needed, for safety to earn.

The umbilical cord wrapped around tight,
In her child's neck, causing a fright.
A heart-wrenching choice, she faced the test,
Only one may survive, they did their best.

With strength unmatched, she braved the storm,
Delivered a son, her dreams reborn.
Yet joy was mingled with a heavy plight,
Complications arose in the still of the night.

Fat leakage troubled her healing wounds,
Her stitches opened, the pain resumed.
Fifteen days in, with blood seeping out,
Another surgery followed, her fears about.

Her recovery fraught with hurdles to clear,
But she pressed on, for the son she held dear.
When jaundice struck at eight months of age,
Breastfeeding ceased, a silent rage.
Day and night, she watched with care,
For her child's health, she'd never despair.
Sleepless nights and weary days,
She stood by him in all possible ways.

Her path was marred by endless trials,
Yet she faced each one with steadfast smiles.
Her son's fragile state tested her heart,
But she held him close, never to part.

In the quiet hours, she whispered a prayer,
For strength and courage to face each care.
Though her body ached and her spirit wore thin,
She found her resolve deep within.

The nights were long, her rest too brief,
Yet for her child, she set aside her grief.
Through moments of doubt and pangs of pain,
Her love for her son never did wane.

Doctors' visits, a familiar scene,
Hoping for news that offered serene.
Yet each challenge brought a new fight,
As she navigated through darkness and light.

In the midst of her own healing plight,
She stayed vigilant, both day and night.
Her hands to comfort, her heart to mend,
A mother's journey, her love without end.
Through trials unknown and fears untold,
She stood by him, a love so bold.
For her son's future, she'd pay any price,
Her devotion unwavering, her sacrifice.

As the days turned to weeks, she found her way,
A mother's resolve in each step of the day.
Though her path was steep, she held on tight,
Guided by the bond that burned so bright.

Her journey a testament to courage and love,
A mother and son, blessed from above.
For in her endurance, her strength did shine,
A mother's love, resilient and divine.

A Mother's Journey: Love and Sacrifice

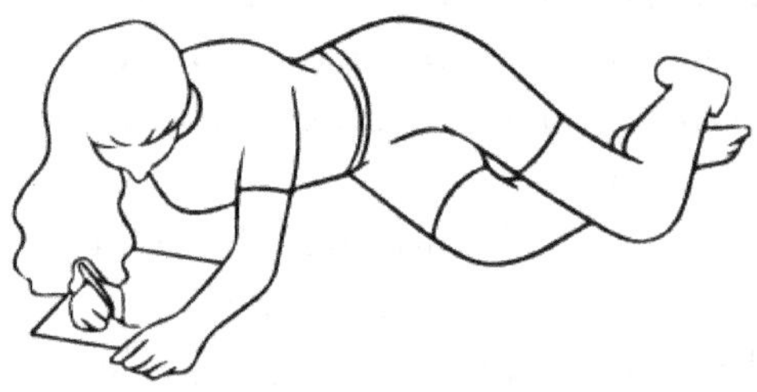

With a heavy heart and a steely will,
She knew she had to work, her resolve instilled.
To support her husband and share the weight,
She stepped into the world to change their fate.

She pursued her BEd, with focus so clear,
Determined to succeed, without fear.
A dream school awaited, her goal in sight,
Where her son could thrive, his future bright.

In her new role, she shone with grace,
Guiding young minds, a nurturing embrace.
Her classroom a haven, where dreams could grow,
A place of learning, a life she did sow.

Yet balancing both work and home,
Required a strength she had never known.
Her days began early, her nights ran late,
In every moment, she carried the weight.

She managed her lessons and household
demands,
A seamless dance, her days in her hands.
Her home a place of warmth and care,
Her son's bright future, her heart's affair.

Though fatigue settled in her weary bones,
She never complained, her courage shown.
For her son's education, she'd do it all,
A mother's love answering the call.

Her mornings began with the rise of the sun,
Preparing for the day before it had begun.
She juggled her duties with tireless grace,
A mother's resilience, her heart's embrace.

In the schoolroom, she gave her all,
Guiding her students to stand tall.
A dream fulfilled, her passion alive,
Nurturing young minds, helping them thrive.

Then home to her family, where love would
meet,
A second round of work, a mother's feat.

Cooking and cleaning, tending with care,
Her spirit unwavering, her love always there.

Her son's laughter, a melody sweet,
Echoed through halls, her day complete.
Though her journey was often a trial,
Her sacrifices were worth every mile.

Her husband's support a pillar strong,
Together they faced the day head-on.
In their shared dreams, they found their way,
Navigating life, come what may.

The weight of the world she carried with pride,
Her son's future, her guiding light.
Though the days were long and the nights the
same,
Her love for her family a burning flame.

Through each challenge, she found her strength,
A testament to her love's true length.
Her heart full of dreams, her soul full of song,
A mother's journey, resilient and strong.

Dreams in the Quiet of Her Heart

In her heart, she held a secret desire,
To be a housewife, tending to the hearth's fire.
To be there always, her home to tend,
A life of quiet moments, a journey without end.

The thought of days spent with her son,
Watching him grow under the sun,
Filling her home with love and care,
Her deepest dream, beyond compare.

Yet she knew the path she must take,
For her son's future, the choice she would make.
A working woman, she embraced the call,
To give her son the best of all.

Her sacrifice, a silent ache,

As she balanced both roles for her son's sake.
Her love a beacon, guiding her way,
Through each challenge, every day.

Though her heart yearned for a simpler time,
She knew her work was her life's climb.
For in her son's eyes, she saw her dream,
His future bright, her life's true beam.
Her journey paved with love and might,
To build a world where he could take flight.
Though she longed for a slower pace,
Her choices forged with quiet grace.

For her family, she gave her best,
Finding strength in her dual quest.
Her love a guiding, unbreakable thread,
A mother's devotion, wherever it led.

Through moments of longing and bittersweet
tears,
She pressed on, setting aside her fears.
Her dreams woven with duty and love,
Her sacrifice a blessing from above.

In quiet moments, she would dream,
Of simpler days by a peaceful stream.
To sit at home and cook with care,
The warmth of the kitchen, her heart laid bare.

The scent of tea wafting through,
A moment of calm, a dream come true.
Decorating her home with thoughtful grace,
Creating a haven, a sacred space.

She longed to go for walks in the sun,
The freedom of nature, a race to be run.
Planting trees with her hands in the soil,
Watching them grow, her heart's quiet toil.

In her dreams, she saw herself dance,
Moving with joy, lost in the trance.
The rhythm of life in each graceful stride,
Her soul alive, her spirit open wide.

These simple pleasures she yearned to find,
Moments of peace for her weary mind.
Yet her path was chosen, her role defined,
A working mother, her heart intertwined.

Though these desires tugged at her soul,
She knew her mission, her ultimate goal.
For her son's future, she made the choice,
Setting aside her dreams, her inner voice.

Yet hope remained in her tender heart,
That one day soon, she could play her part.
To embrace her dreams with a joyful cheer,
As her son's journey would soon be clear.

For now, she nurtures the seeds of her dreams,
Patiently waiting for her life's flowing streams.
With love as her anchor, she holds on tight,
A mother's journey, a path so bright.

Dual Realities: The Teacher and the Home

When the world changed in an instant's blink,
Her husband's work was brought to the brink.
With businesses shuttered, a silence so deep,
Her family's needs, a promise to keep.

She took on the burden with a heavy heart,
Becoming the man of the family, her part.
To bear the expenses, to carry the load,
She stepped up to face a challenging road.

Through uncertainty, she held her ground,
Navigating change with resolve profound.
She worked tirelessly to keep them afloat,
A mother's strength, an unbreakable coat.

Long nights and days stretched far and wide,
Yet she pressed on with unwavering pride.
Her love for her family, a guiding force,
Through darkened paths, she stayed the course.

Her husband beside her, his heart filled with
pain,
Unable to work, he felt the strain.
Yet she reassured him with a gentle touch,
Together they faced the trials as such.
Her sacrifices multiplied, but so did her hope,
Her dreams deferred, yet she found ways to
cope.
For the sake of her son, her family's light,
She fought each battle, holding on tight.

Though times were tough and worries were
great,
She faced each challenge, accepting her fate.
A mother, a warrior, her spirit unbowed,
Her love for her family declared aloud.

Amidst the shifting tides of change,
She had to adapt, her world rearranged.
Online classes now became her quest,
To teach and guide while giving her best.

Her home transformed, a classroom space,
A place of learning, a sacred base.
Setting up screens and adjusting the light,
To create an environment both warm and bright.

Lessons planned, her voice steady and clear,
Reaching her students, though they weren't near.
Through virtual halls, she shared her heart,
Teaching her passion, imparting her art.

Yet beyond the screen, her household called,
Her duties as mother and wife installed.
Meals to prepare, rooms to maintain,
Balancing it all, she bore the strain.

She moved with grace, from task to task,
Wearing many hats, behind a steadfast mask.
Her time divided, yet her spirit intact,
A juggling act of both work and pact.

Late nights spent grading and planning,
Early mornings with her home demanding.
But she found her rhythm, a careful dance,
In this new reality, she took her stance.

Her strength shone through her every stride,
Managing both worlds, side by side.
For her family and students, she gave her all,
A mother and teacher, answering the call.

In the face of upheaval, she persevered,
Through dedication and love, her path cleared.
Her resilience a light in uncertain times,
A mother's journey, her devotion sublime.

Through the trials of COVID, she became their
shield,
Her determination and courage revealed.
A beacon of hope in uncertain days,
A mother's strength, her guiding ways.

Echoes of Absence: A Daughter's Grief

The world stood still as her heart grew cold,
The news of her mother, a loss untold.
The pain of separation, a heavy weight,
Unable to see her, bound by fate.

In the grip of a pandemic's tight hold,
She was kept apart, her grief controlled.
No chance to say goodbye, no final embrace,
Her mother's absence, an empty space.

Tears uncried, a sorrow she bore,
Longing for her mother's touch once more.
The ache of loss, a wound so deep,
In her quiet moments, she'd silently weep.

The world's restrictions kept her at bay,
From bidding farewell, she was led astray.
Her mother's love now out of reach,
A grief unspoken, with no words to teach.

The trauma of loss in isolation,
A pain she carried, her quiet devastation.
Through this ordeal, she moved with care,
Her heart still burdened, a heavy stare.
The loss of her anchor, a mother's love,
Left her adrift, her spirit above.
Yet she found her strength in memories held,
In her mother's wisdom, her heart swelled.

Though the days were dark and her soul was
low,
She clung to the love her mother bestowed.
The pain of absence, a lasting sting,
Yet her mother's voice in her heart would sing.

She faced the grief with silent resolve,
Finding her way as the days evolved.
In her mother's honor, she kept the fight,
Her journey of love, a guiding light.

Resilience in Transformation: A Journey to Self-Care

In the wake of her trials, she turned the page,
A journey of healing, a new chapter to wage.
Determined and focused, she found her way,
To care for herself each passing day.

She shed the weight of her physical frame,
Through effort and strength, she played the game.
Gym sessions of two hours, every day she'd give,
Her willpower steadfast, her spirit to live.

She chose her meals with thoughtful care,
Avoiding carbs, a disciplined affair.

For a year she persevered, her goals in sight,
Her journey one of self-love and might.

The world watched as she transformed,
But whispers and taunts she often endured.
Their words could sting, yet she held on tight,
Her heart set on her path, her future bright.

Despite the comments and the doubtful eyes,
She stayed the course, reaching for the skies.
Each pound lost, a victory won,
Her journey of strength had just begun.

In the face of adversity, she stood her ground,
Refusing to let negativity abound.
Her courage unwavering, her heart set free,
She found herself, her own victory.

As the days turned to weeks and months to
years,
She saw her progress, her doubts cleared.
Her goals achieved through struggle and pain,
A testament to her resolve, her journey not in
vain.

Her reflection now showed her fight,
A story of triumph, her journey alight.
She found herself in each step she took,
A path of resilience, a brand-new book.

Hidden Burdens, Unspoken Strength

In the midst of her personal strife,
She carried the weight of her family's life.
Financial burdens she took in stride,
For her husband and home, she did not hide.

Household expenses she managed with grace,
Making ends meet, a delicate chase.
She navigated travel with careful thought,
Booking journeys, with challenges fraught.

Hotel bills and clothing needs,
She met each one, planting new seeds.
Looking out for her husband's kin,
Providing care, a duty within.

Medical expenses, a heavy toll,
She bore it all with a mother's soul.
Yet her efforts, often unseen,
Were taken for granted, a silent scream.

Her innocence, a vulnerability worn,
Used by others, leaving her torn.
She gave her all, her heart so pure,
But recognition was seldom sure.
Through all her sacrifices, she remained,
A pillar of strength, her love unchained.
Yet the lack of appreciation weighed,
As she continued on, her heart betrayed.

In her giving, she found no end,
Her family's needs she did attend.
Yet the pain of being overlooked,
Was a burden she silently undertook.

Despite it all, she pressed ahead,
Her soul resilient, her spirit widespread.
For her loved ones, she'd pay the price,
Though her kindness often came at a sacrifice.

Her journey of strength intertwined with sorrow,
Yet she faced each new tomorrow.
For her family's well-being, she would fight,
A mother's love shining ever so bright.

Trust Tested: A Mother's Quiet Strength

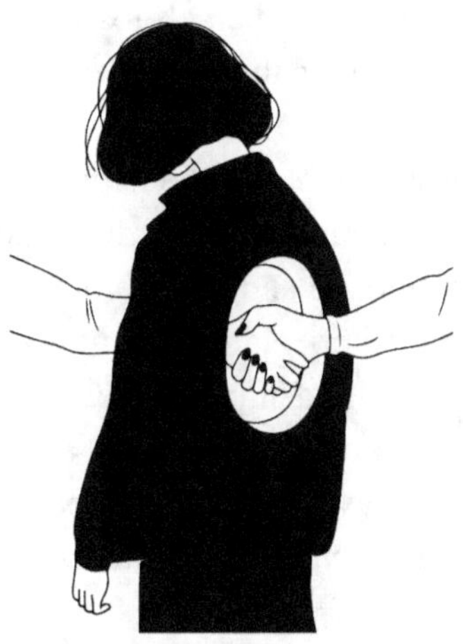

Her trust was fragile, yet she held on tight,
Giving chances, despite her own plight.
Again and again, she forgave and tried,
Though her self-esteem she could not hide.

The pain of betrayal cut deep in her soul,
Yet she endured, playing her role.
Hoping for change, for love to be shown,
But often her hopes were left alone.

No hand to guide her, no warmth to share,
Her needs unattended, her heart laid bare.
She walked to the hospital, self-care in hand,

Facing each visit, on her own she would stand.

In her moments of quiet despair,
She purchased gifts, her own self to care.
A token of love, from herself to she,
A solace for wounds that others couldn't see.

Her spirit was tested, yet she kept her grace,
A mother's endurance, her burdens she'd face.
Though overlooked and often ignored,
Her heart stayed open, her love never bored.
Through all the hardships, her resilience shone,
A light in the darkness, she faced all alone.
Her trust may have wavered, her pain so real,
But her heart remained open, her soul to heal.

She chose to rise above the dismay,
Holding on to hope, day by day.
For in her strength, she found her way,
A mother's love, her guiding ray.

Though life dealt her trials untold,
She pressed on, her spirit bold.
Her journey of strength, her self-love refined,
A testament to the power of a mother's mind.

Harbors of Hope:
Friendship's Embrace

In her darkest days, her heart heavy with woe,
Two friends emerged, like stars in the snow.
Their trust unwavering, their support so deep,
They held her close when she needed to weep.

Through thick and thin, they stood by her side,
A steadfast presence, her true friends and guide.
They listened to her fears, her silent cries,
Offering comfort, a place she could confide.

Their laughter echoed through her soul,
A balm for her wounds, making her whole.
They danced with her in moments of cheer,
Turning sorrows to smiles, wiping away tears.

Songs shared with joy, voices lifted high,
In harmony, they touched the sky.
In friendship's embrace, they found their way,
Lighting her path, keeping the darkness at bay.

When life's burdens seemed too much to bear,
They reminded her she wasn't alone in despair.
Their trust a sanctuary, a place of respite,
Helping her find her own strength and might.

In her friends' hearts, she found a home,
A place where her spirit could freely roam.
Their kindness a beacon in troubled seas,
Guiding her through life's complexities.

Their laughter and love filled her days,
Turning her journey into a dance of praise.
For in their friendship, she found relief,
A reminder that she was never in grief.

Together they faced the world as one,
Their bond a shelter, a journey begun.
With their support, she could rise and stand,
Her two true friends, her safe harbor on land.

Dreams Reclaimed: A Journey with Family

In her journey of trials, her dreams pushed aside,
Her brother and bhabhi emerged as her guide.
A beacon of strength, a light in her night,
They offered her solace, her dreams in sight.

With open arms, they reached out to her,
A sanctuary of love, in which she could stir.
They lifted her up when she needed a hand,
Helping her find the courage to stand.

In their presence, she found her reprieve,
A place of warmth where she could believe.
They knew her heart, her desires untold,
Their support a comfort, a story unrolled.

Together, they encouraged her to soar,
To chase her dreams, to seek for more.
They took her away from the weight of despair,
A fresh start, a chance for her heart to repair.

Her brother's wisdom, her bhabhi's care,
Their guidance a treasure, beyond compare.
In their embrace, she found her way,
To live her dreams, to find a new day.
They reminded her she deserved the best,
To follow her heart, to embrace the quest.
Through their support, she found her voice,
A renewed strength, a reason to rejoice.

Their love an anchor, their presence a balm,
A sanctuary of peace, a place of calm.
With their support, she could see the light,
To pursue her passions, to reach new heights.

In their strength, she found her own,
A place where her true self could be shown.
Her brother and bhabhi, her guiding stars,
Helping her heal, from near and afar.

Together they journeyed, a path of dreams,
Where love and support flowed like streams.
With their guidance, she found her way,
A new chapter dawned, her soul at play.

The Mystery Guardian

In the tapestry of her life's long quest,
An unknown hand reached out to invest.
A mystery figure, unseen yet near,
Whose quiet support erased her fear.

This guardian angel, a guiding light,
Helped her navigate through day and night.
Though his identity remains untold,
His presence a comfort, a bond of gold.

With each step she takes, his shadow remains,
A gentle presence that eases her pains.
His silent wisdom, a soft embrace,
Guiding her through each uncertain space.

His support like a whisper, a breeze so kind,
Lifting her spirits, clearing her mind.
Through highs and lows, he's walked unseen,
His faith in her journey a hope serene.

Though she may never know his name,
His impact on her life is clear as flame.
A mystery companion on her path anew,
Helping her dreams and her strength accrue.

His role a secret, his touch so dear,
But in his care, she has nothing to fear.
For in his quiet support, she's found her way,
To live her dreams, to seize each day.

As she moves forward, her heart at ease,
Grateful for the unknown, like leaves in the
breeze.
Her journey now one of courage and might,
With unseen support, she shines so bright.

So she walks on with a grateful heart,
For the unknown ally who played his part.
In her new journey, she feels his care,
A mystery guardian, always there.

Wanderlust's Embrace

In the quiet hum of dawn's first light,
She dreams of roads and skies in flight,
A compass heart, a wanderer's soul,
In the world's vast arms, she finds her goal.

Through bustling cities, past whispering trees,
She dances with the morning breeze,
Mountains call, rivers sing,
She's boundless, untamed, in love with
everything.

Her feet have traced the desert's edge,
Walked the cliffs where oceans pledge,
To meet the sky in a lover's embrace,
She finds her peace in every place.

From Dubai's heights to Singapore's night,
In India's spiritual sanctuaries' light,
In Shimla's cool, Manali's charm,
She feels the world's warm, welcoming arm.

She hears the stories in the wind,
Of ancient paths and dreams unpinned,
Her heart, a map of places gone,
Her soul, a song forever drawn.
In each new dawn, a chance to see,
The world in its vast mystery,
She travels not to escape or flee,
But to weave her life with destiny.

For in her journey, life blooms,
A thousand memories, a hundred rooms,
She's found her love in earth's embrace,
In every mile, in every place.

Her laughter echoes, wild and free,
In the whispering leaves of a foreign tree,
And in her eyes, a story told,
Of a woman whose heart is brave and bold.

She is the sunset on a distant shore,
The morning mist, the lion's roar,
A spirit vast, as old as time,
In every land, she finds her rhyme.

So let her roam, let her be,
A voyager in eternity,
For she has found her life's sweet grace,
In the endless beauty of every place.

Rebirth of a Radiant Soul

In shadows deep, she once did dwell,
A silent heart with stories to tell,
But dawn has kissed her weary eyes,
And she rises now, where hope lies.

She casts aside the weight of night,
Embraces dawn, her spirit bright,
In mirrors, she sees not the past,
But a future, fierce and vast.

With care, she drapes a vibrant saree,
Elegance in every pleat, set free,
Or sometimes, in a kurta's flow,
Her beauty shines, her spirits glow.

She lines her eyes with kohl so dark,
A gaze that leaves a lasting mark,
Adorns her wrists with bangles bright,
In gold and glass, a shimmering light.

Her earrings jingle, small and grand,
In intricate designs, by skilled hand,
A bindi placed with utmost grace,
A final touch upon her face.

She braids her hair or lets it fall,
In every style, she stands tall,
With henna patterns on her skin,
A celebration deep within.

She grooms herself with tender care,
A radiant beauty, beyond compare,
Her laughter rings, a joyful sound,
In gatherings where love is found.

She mingles, dances, sings with cheer,
Embracing life, shedding fear,
Her steps are light, her heart is free,
She moves with newfound liberty.

In every glance, in every smile,
She finds her strength, her unique style,
Her voice, once quiet, now takes flight,

In songs that echo through the night.

Melodies of joy and pain,
Of a spirit unchained, free from strain,
She meets the world with open arms,
Reclaims her place, her vibrant charms.

A woman reborn, fierce and true,
She's discovered life anew,
With every heartbeat, every breath,
She celebrates her own rebirth.
Her story now, a tale of grace,
Of finding light in darkest place,
A testament to strength untold,
A woman's heart, brave and bold.

Her Terms, Her Life

In shadows cast by rigid norms,
She longed to break free, to transform,
A spirit caged by old ideals,
Her heart yearned for what was real.

She rose against the binding tide,
Cast off the weight she felt inside,
Orthodox whispers, cold and grey,
She brushed aside, found her own way.

No longer bound by customs' chains,
She danced in the sun and welcomed rains,
In saree or in jeans, she wore,
Her soul's own truth, and nothing more.

She lined her eyes with kohl so bold,

A fire within that can't be sold,
Adorned her wrists with bangles bright,
But only if they felt just right.

She spoke her mind with fearless grace,
No longer hid behind a face,
That others painted, masked and veiled,
Her own true voice, now loud, prevailed.

She chose her path, with steps so light,
Unfazed by judgments, day or night,
She walked in freedom, head held high,
A gleam of defiance in her eye.

In gatherings where whispers flew,
She stood her ground, she stayed true,
To dreams and visions, her own call,
A woman unbowed, standing tall.

Her choices, once a silent scream,
Now lived out loud, a vivid dream,
She met the world on her own terms,
A force of nature, passion burns.

No longer shadowed by the past,
She forged a future bright and vast,
A testament to strength untamed,
A woman's power, unashamed.

In every laugh, in every breath,
She celebrated life and death,
The orthodox fell far behind,
She lived by heart, free in her mind.

Her story now, a song of fire,
Of breaking free, of rising higher,
A beacon for those yet to see,
The beauty of living fearlessly.

Her Own Standard

In a world where whispers often say,
A woman needs a man to find her way,
She stands apart, her own life's queen,
A sovereign spirit, fierce and keen.

She wakes to mornings soft and bright,
Her own company, her pure delight,
With dreams that span the open sky,
She finds her strength, learns to fly.

No knight in armor by her side,
She walks alone with steady stride,
Her standards high, her heart so true,
She knows her worth in all she'll do.

In every task, in every goal,
She pours her heart, her very soul,
No need for someone to complete,
A life so rich, so pure, replete.

She crafts her world with hands so sure,
A realm of peace, a spirit pure,
Her laughter rings through empty halls,
Her joy a light, her voice a call.

She sets her table, one fine place,
With elegance, with style and grace,
Her meals a feast of dreams and care,
A celebration she can share.

With friends she dances, sings her song,
In her own rhythm, she belongs,
No need for validation's mark,
She shines alone, a glowing spark.

Her standards high, she will not bend,
For any lover or pretend,
She knows the love she's built within,
A treasure, rare, a priceless gem.

For any man to join her path,
He must respect her inner wrath,
Her strength, her wisdom, fierce and bright,
Her standards set, her guiding light.

He must embrace her wild heart,
Her freedom, every intricate part,
For she's a woman, whole and free,
Her love a gift, her soul the key.

No settling for less than she,
Deserves in love, her destiny,
A partner who will stand beside,
Not one to tame, nor one to guide.

Her story, one of strength and grace,
A journey in her own sweet pace,
A woman's life, complete, profound,
In self-love's arms, she's truly found.

The Heart of Home

In the quiet of the morning light,
She finds her joy, her heart's delight,
A housewife's path, her chosen way,
In love and care, she starts her day.

Her hands weave magic through each room,
With flowers fresh, a soft perfume,
She decorates with tender care,
A home that breathes in every air.

The curtains drawn, the sunlight streams,
She crafts her world from woven dreams,
Each pillow placed, each picture hung,
A song of home that's always sung.

In garden green, she spends her time,

Where roses climb and jasmine twine,
Her fingers tend to earth and seed,
A blooming life, her heart's true need.

She kneels beside the budding rows,
With gentle hands, her garden grows,
The vibrant hues, the fragrant air,
A testament to all her care.

In kitchen warm, she stirs and bakes,
With every dish, her love she makes,
A symphony of scents and taste,
No effort spared, no moment a waste.

From simmering pots to bread's warm rise,
She cooks with love, a sweet surprise,
Each meal a gift, each table set,
In every bite, her care is met.

Her apron tied, her hair pulled back,
She finds her rhythm, keeps her track,
In simple acts, her joy is found,
A life in love and laughter bound.

Her heart's content, her spirit light,
In every chore, she finds delight,
A housewife proud, her life her own,
In every space, her love has grown.

For in her home, she builds her dreams,
In quiet moments, soft sunbeams,
She finds her place, her world, her part,
A life lived fully from the heart.

So here she stands, in peace and grace,
A smile alight upon her face,
Her happy heart, her gentle hands,
Create a home where love expands.

True Joys in Simple Days

She left behind the gilded walls,
The masquerade of lavish halls,
A life of pretense, grand façade,
She sought the truth, the real, the raw.

She stepped into the vibrant street,
Where life and laughter often meet,
In the hum of local trains, she found,
A rhythm pure, a grounded sound.

No longer bound by show and pride,
She walked with freedom, open-eyed,
In bustling markets, colors bright,
She felt her spirit taking flight.

The scent of spices filled the air,
Street food delights beyond compare,
From samosas crisp to chaat's sweet zest,

In every bite, she found her quest.

She traveled in the crowded bus,
In shared warmth, no needless fuss,
Conversations rich with stories spun,
In every face, a life begun.

She bartered with the street-side sellers,
For trinkets bright and hand-woven treasures,
Each purchase, small but filled with grace,
A connection to a simpler place.

Her days were filled with humble joys,
With simple sights and common ploys,
She found a wealth in what's unseen,
In moments small, in places mean.

Gone were the days of empty show,
Her heart embraced life's ebb and flow,
She danced in the rain, laughed in the sun,
A journey true, a life begun.

In every corner of the street,
She found a world, diverse, complete,
A tapestry of human touch,
A life that she had missed so much.

She felt the earth beneath her feet,
In every lane, in every greet,

She lived each day with earnest cheer,
Her heart sincere, her mind clear.

No longer masked by false display,
She cherished every simple day,
A woman free, in middle class stride,
With open heart, and eyes wide.

Her story now, a tale of grace,
Of finding joy in commonplace,
A testament to life's sweet art,
Of living fully, from the heart.

The Enchantress of Light and Love

In the tapestry of night and day,
She dances with a light display,
Her laughter like a lilting song,
Enchanting hearts as she moves along.

With eyes that sparkle, wide and bright,
She sees the beauty in each sight,
In every soul she meets anew,
She finds a charm, a grace, a hue.

Her words, like honey, sweet and clear,
Draw people close, bring joy and cheer,
A flirt, a tease, yet pure and kind,
She leaves a trail of smiles behind.

She loves to live, she loves to play,
Her spirit like a sunny ray,
Extroverted, bold, and free,
Yet she knows where her bounds should be.

In every glance, in every touch,
She shows she cares, but not too much,
She flirts with life, she flirts with fate,
But true love's flame, she'll never sate.

For in her heart, a dream resides,
Of one true love, where she confides,
A soulmate, rare, and deeply known,
A love that's hers, and hers alone.

She dances through the ebb and flow,
With grace and charm, she lets it show,
Appreciating all she sees,
Yet holding close her tender keys.

To love, to laugh, to flirt with ease,
To find the beauty, to appease,
She's a woman of the night and day,
Her spirit free, her heart in sway.

A Story Still Incomplete

Through trials deep and sorrows past,
She walked a path, alone at last,
A marriage lost, a chapter closed,
Yet in her heart, a hope still grows.

With courage fierce, she raised her child,
Through stormy nights and mornings mild,
A single mother, strong and true,
She built a life from what she knew.

But whispers of her longing heart,
Tell tales of dreams that won't depart,
For love that heals, for touch divine,
A soul to blend with hers, entwined.

Her story, though, is far from done,
A journey bright beneath the sun,
For though she's known both joy and pain,
The final lines have yet to gain.

They say her heart should find its peace,
With love to make her burdens cease,
A partner kind, a bond so sweet,
To make her life feel more complete.

But she, with spirit wild and free,
Knows life's a dance, a mystery,
And while she dreams of love's embrace,
She seeks adventure, finds her place.

Her laughter echoes through the air,
She lives with grace beyond compare,
In every smile, in every stride,
She carries hope, her faithful guide.

A story still in bloom, she stands,
With open heart and outstretched hands,
For life's true love, for dreams replete,
A tale of strength, yet incomplete.

For in her soul, a fire burns bright,
To chase the dawn, to kiss the night,
Her journey's end, yet to be told,
A story rich, still to unfold.